Hilary Townsend was born into a Blackmore Vale farming family, spending her childhood at Hewletts Farm and Thornhill, near Stalbridge. She became a personnel manager in industry, then a lecturer in management subjects at Frome Technical College, while writing about Dorset as a hobby. Made redundant when the college closed, she was able, after years of homesickness, to return to the Blackmore Vale and write full time. A passionate conservationist who has spent many years restoring her medieval house in Stalbridge, she now writes about this work, especially for North American publications. She has done broadcasts for the BBC on her childhood and William Barnes, and is well-known as a lecturer on the Blackmore Vale and its traditions.

Following page
The Blackmore Vale south of Bishop's Caundle:
narrow lanes with wide verges and sturdy hedgerow oaks.

DISCOVER DORSET

BLACKMORE VALE

HILARY TOWNSEND

THE DOVECOTE PRESS

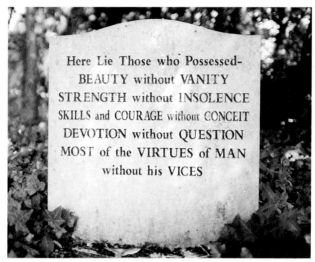

The memorial to seven hounds, buried nearby,
in Stock Gaylard churchyard.

First published in 2004 by The Dovecote Press Ltd
Stanbridge, Wimborne, Dorset BH21 4JD

ISBN I 904349 34 X

Typeset in Monotype Sabon
Printed and bound by Baskerville Press, Salisbury, Wiltshire

All papers used by The Dovecote Press are natural, recyclable products made
from wood grown in sustainable, well-managed forests

A CIP catalogue record for this book is available
from the British Library

1 3 5 7 9 8 6 4 2

CONTENTS

FINDING THE BLACKMORE VALE

There we could see green vields at hand,
Avore a hunderd on beyand,
An' rows o' trees in hedges roun'
Green meäds, an' zummerleäzes brown,
An' thorns upon the zunny down,
While air, vrom the rocken zedge
In brook, did come along the hedge,
Where we did keep our flagon

'Where We Did Keep Our Flagon', WILLIAM BARNES

You are about to get to know one of the loveliest stretches of countryside the British Isles can show you, but before you can do so we have to find it. And the best way to do this is to climb the surrounding hills and look down.

Monica Hutchings did so in her book *Dorset River*, published in 1956. She was following the course of the River Stour from its mouth at Christchurch and had driven from Blandford to Bulbarrow, then she climbed the high ridge of Shillingstone Hill. Actually, she did more than climb the hill, she stood on the roof of her car. From this vantage point she could see the Blackmore Vale over Hod and Hambledon Hills across to Alfred's Tower, wooded Duncliffe and miles of the valley of the River Stour spread out below her.

Thomas Hardy, writing *Tess of the D'Urbervilles* in the 1890's, came up from the coast over a 'bold chalk ridge', a line of chalk hills that bounds the Vale on the south side. Here he saw 'a fertile and

Opposite Contrasting views of the Blackmore Vale.
Top Looking north from below Bulbarrow.
Bottom Boating on the River Stour at Sturminster Newton,
one of a group of photographs taken by William Barnes' son in 1883.

[7]

sheltered tract of country where the fields are never brown and the springs never run dry, where the fields are mere paddocks and from this height their hedgerows appear a network of darkly green threads overspreading the pale green of the grass'.

Sir Frederick Treves in his classic *Highways and Byways in Dorset*, published in 1906, tells us that the traveller who climbs to the crest of the Dorset heights, between Nettlecombe Tout and Bulbarrow, 'can survey the whole county from Mere to the Purbeck hills. The land lying Northwards – the blue-misted hinterland – is rich, luxuriant and fair to see, a cavalier country of flocks and herds, and of many trees.' There are fewer trees, Dutch elm disease has seen to that, but if you stand on Bulbarrow on a frosty midwinter morning you will see the crowns of clumps of evergreen trees, or perhaps deciduous trees covered with ivy, arising in the Vale as the mist clears.

The Blackmore Vale though, for all that it has the River Stour running through it, is not simply a wide clay valley. It has many hills rising within it. On one of these is Stalbridge where I live, a small town a few miles from Sherborne. Here you can find the Post Office in the High Street, then walk up a hill behind it called Barrow Hill. After less than ten minutes' walk you will find on your right the Jubilee Seat set into the wall of Stalbridge Park and commemorating the Silver Jubilee of King George V.

With the seat behind you, face Hardy's 'bold chalk ridge', the escarpment of the Dorset North Downs, and you will see prehistoric Hambledon Hill, then to the right Bell Hill, Woolland Hill, Bulbarrow (with its two masts pointing skyward which began life in the Second World Ward as 'Radio Location Posts'), Church Hill and Ridge Hill.

After that Dogbury Gate, High Stoy and Batcombe Hill might be visible if it is an exceptionally clear day and you have powerful field glasses. In any case, you are now looking back at Hardy's view of the Vale so wave to his ghost up there, a slight, tweed clad, heavily moustached figure with an Edwardian bicycle.

The Blackmore Vale to the east is bounded by Cranborne Chase and follows the line of the A350 road from Ranston Hill and on through the villages of Iwerne Minster, Fontmell Magna and Compton Abbas, West Melbury and Cann. We shall now skirt lightly around Shaftesbury on the south side, because the town of Shaftesbury, for all

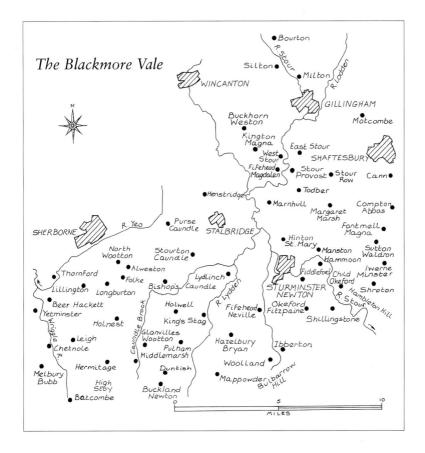

The Blackmore Vale

its noble prominence 800 feet above the Vale, is omitted, as is Sherborne, because we are going to discover the essentially rural Blackmore Vale.

The northern boundary of the Vale stretches almost like a jaunty jester's cap above Gillingham through Motcombe to Queen Oak and Bourton, then crosses the A303, ignores the A30 and slips down on winding country roads past Bow Brook and Gibbs Marsh towards Sherborne.

Once again I would beg the traveller on this journey of discovery to look down on the Vale from high places, from Shaftesbury towards Sherborne Causeway over scenery of heart-stopping beauty, to stand in the churchyard at Kington Magna and absorb the fieldscape below, or to drive (better still, walk) to the top of Wincanton High Street, turn right into Bayford Road and go through Bayford where you will see most arrestingly lovely views across the Vale to your right.

We now have only the western boundary to define, but it is easy to find. You drive south of Sherborne down attractively named Dancing Hill, go across the A352 (which would if you followed it instead of crossing it, take you to Middlemarsh) and pick up the line of the River Yeo towards Beer Hackett, Yetminster and Chetnole. On signposts off to your right you will see lyrical Dorset place-names such as Ryme Intrinseca and Melbury Bubb. Our western boundary ends below Chetnole at Newlands Farm.

You now have breathtaking views across the Vale, for you are near Dogbury Gate and Ridge Hill, which were, you remember, part of Thomas Hardy's 'bold chalk escarpment' where we began our quest. So, now having defined the boundaries, we are going to plunge down into the heart of the Blackmore Vale to discover for ourselves the Vale's incredible richness. Everything about it is rich. Seams of rich Oxford clay run through it giving it good grass and therefore excellent dairy farming (though sheep thrive on the hills). Big trees flourish there. They flourished in dense forests of course, until the movement to carve out farms and various Kings' need for hearts of oak for their navies put an end to that.

All the same isolated big trees – oak, ash and horse chestnuts – are found everywhere. Growing good quality timber requires large supplies of water. The trees get it from springs everywhere, in the hills and in the floor of the Vale, which in turn feed the little brooks – the Divelish, Lydden, Caundle Brook, Cale, Lodden, Shreen Water, Bibberne. The very names are melodious. These in turn feed into the slowly meandering River Stour, the true source of all the Blackmore Vale's richness.

DISCOVERING THE PAST

To understand the ancient Blackmore Vale we need to know how it grew and developed to be what we see today. Early Iron Age settlers developed fortresses, notably on Hod Hill and Hambledon Hill, which were strengthened with ditches and ramparts, until Vespasian's Second Augustan Legion battered their way into them and conquered the native tribes.

After that Roman influence spread all over the Vale and is still being uncovered. In 1897 General Pitt Rivers started an extensive excavation of Roman buildings half a mile north of Iwerne Minster, and a Roman corpse buried with a coin in his mouth (to pay the

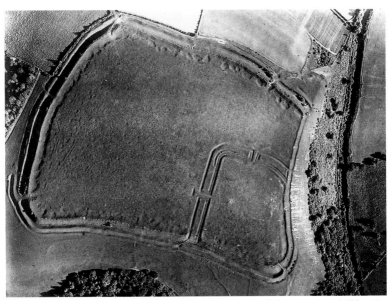

Hod Hill from the air. In the bottom right corner of the Iron Age hillfort is the Roman fort, built to station a cohort of the 2nd Legion and a cavalry regiment after the Roman conquest of Dorset in 43 AD.

ferryman to carry him into the underworld) was dug up during the building of a milk factory in Stalbridge in the First World War.

The most remarkable discovery though was at Hinton St. Mary, near Sturminster Newton. A blacksmith putting in a gate post in 1963 came upon the beautiful mosaic floor of a Roman villa, complete with a pattern round the edges of running dogs pursuing and bringing down stags. And in the middle there was an early representation of the head of Christ. The blacksmith had studied Roman Christian mosaics during war service in Italy and, as he uncovered the floor that day, he recognized the extraordinary importance of what he had found. This exceptional find is now housed in the British Museum.

After the Romans left, from about AD 430, Saxon raiding parties surged into the Blackmore Vale, then settled in Wessex. They clustered around their chiefs and settled in farmland newly won from forest clearings, ploughing the land in strips. They built churches such as the minster at Iwerne Minster (though the present church is largely Norman). Todber near Gillingham has a cross in the church made up of Saxon pieces. They were accomplished craftsmen, especially in glass and gold, and it was said that Saxon Wessex enjoyed a high degree of civilization and peace.

However, from the eighth century, the peace of civilized Saxon Dorset was shattered by ferocious, noisy, freebooting Vikings, attracted to the Wessex of King Alfred by the rich settled farming land. Alfred's courage and skill in driving them out are commemorated by Alfred's Tower (called locally Stourton Tower) on Kingsettle Hill in the woods by the village of Stourton. Erected in 1760 by one of the Hoares of Stourhead on what he considered was the site where the West Saxon army gathered, the tower is 150 feet high. Standing 800 feet above sea level, it is a landmark over the Blackmore Vale for miles around. It is said that Alfred's recruits were gathered where Somerset, Dorset and Wiltshire meet by the simple process of hurling clods of earth at the doors of their homes late at night, to get them mobilised, a custom commemorated in Stalbridge on Pan-shard Night (Shrove Tuesday) till well into the nineteenth century.

Another landmark, though less conspicuous, is Slaughtergate Farm, a name reinforced by the Scandinavian 'gate', to the west of

Above left The head of Christ from the mosaic dining room floor at Hinton St Mary Roman villa. Behind him is the *chi-rho* symbol, the two Greek letters which together form *chr*, the first letters of Christ's name. He is flanked by pomegranates, symbols of eternal life.

Above right The restored Saxon cross-shaft found in Todber church. The shaft, with its lovely interlaced leaf and scroll-work, now stands in the churchyard.

Gillingham. This, by local tradition, is the site of a mass burial of Danes who lost a battle there, probably at the hands of Edmund Ironside in 1016, and the burial mound is now a scheduled ancient monument.

Saxon peace and order were shattered again in 1066 by William of Normandy. His conquest resulted in the building of castles to subdue the defeated English, and the Domesday Survey, a great help to William when taxing them.

William created many forests in his new realm, though his definition of what was a forest included open land as well as woodland. His successors, also passionate about hunting, added greatly to the afforestation of the Blackmore Vale, so that later monarchs were able to present large amounts of timber to churches and religious foundations.

Farms were developed in forest clearings. Gradually tenants agreed with the lord of the manor to enclose for pasture land formerly held in common. At Hinton St. Mary and Gillingham significant enclosures had been carried out by the end of the sixteenth century. Sheep as well as cows grazed in the Blackmore Vale, hemp and flax were grown in its rich soil and the number of mills and quarries recorded adds to our picture of the Vale's industries in the Middle Ages.

How was the Blackmore Vale affected by the Reformation? Shaftesbury Abbey, the wealthiest foundation for women in the country, was dissolved and ruined, with a great loss of revenue for the area from pilgrims and farming. The Abbey at Sherborne was dissolved, but fortunately became and remains the town's parish church. Lands held by the Abbey of Glastonbury in Somerset (another extremely rich foundation), at Sturminster Newton and Buckland Newton, were given over to sheep.

When the monasteries were dissolved they were often bought by men unconnected with the Church. This led to the establishment of new landowning families – especially true in Dorset. One new landowner was the Earl of Cork, Lord Treasurer of Ireland, who in 1636 acquired the Manor and Estate of Stalbridge. The Earl later conveyed this property to his youngest son, the brilliant Robert Boyle (1627-1691).

Robert Boyle was in Europe making the Grand Tour when the Civil War broke out. When he eventually returned in March 1646 it was to find his Stalbridge estate 'greatly decayed' and the whole Blackmore Vale extremely troubled. Cromwell's army had attacked Sherborne, then was forced to march out to Duncliffe and Hambledon to put down the protests of the Clubmen, local people fed up with the damage being done to their crops and homes by both sides.

Once settled in his old home Robert Boyle devoted the next nine years to serious scientific study. He set up his own laboratory and furnace where he could measure the effects of heat, fire, ice and water on common materials. Here he made his early experiments in the compression of air and gave science 'Boyle's Law' relating to gases – that pressures and volume were in reciprocal proportion – work which eventually earned him the title of 'Father of English Chemistry'.

Left 'The Father of English Chemistry', Robert Boyle (1627-1691).

Right The artist Sir James Thornhill (1676-1734).

Because of the work of that solitary, dedicated scientist in the old mansion in Stalbridge Park, we can go deep-sea diving, bore a tunnel through a mountain or drive red-hot bolts into a bridge. We can take a compressor and break up a road and when we've done that we can drive away safely and smoothly on our pneumatic tyres.

Boyle left to live in Oxford and later London, immersing himself in the early work of the Royal Society, but he remained committed to Dorset, styling himself Robert Boyle of Stalbridge in his will and leaving money for a charity school for twenty poor boys at Yetminster. The school has been absorbed into the state system but the buildings remain.

A famous son of the Blackmore Vale in the eighteenth century was the painter Sir James Thornhill. Thornhill, a hamlet a good country mile from Stalbridge, had been recorded in the Domesday Book and by 1227 James Thornhill's family were established as Lords of the Manor there and much respected. The traveller and writer John Leland in the 1540's observed, 'Here dwelleth Master Thornhul, an ancient gentleman'. Sadly, this ancient family fell on hard times and had to sell the Thornhill estate, but James bought it back.

[15]

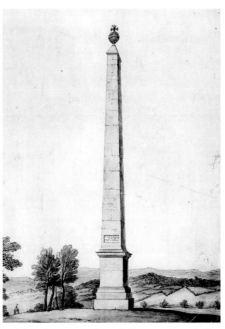

The obelisk erected by Sir James Thornhill near Thornhill House. This is his drawing of the original obelisk, which was 40 feet high and erected in 1727 in honour of George II and Queen Caroline. It was destroyed by a storm in 1836, and the one so prominent today is largely a reconstruction, though it does incorporate much of the original stone.

Thornhill House in the 1950s. Thornhill's family had sold the estate after falling on hard times. Sir James Thornhill bought it back in about 1725, where he built the present house, probably to his own design.

James was born at Melcombe Regis in 1676 and, after a seven year apprenticeship in London, became steadily famous for his work on the Painted Hall at Greenwich, various country houses, including the staircase murals in Sherborne House, royal apartments at Windsor and Hampton Court and, finally, an even greater honour, the dome of St. Paul's Cathedral. He was made 'History Painter' to the King, knighted in 1718 and in 1722 became Member of Parliament for his native Weymouth.

Sir James Thornhill's brilliant career and fortune enabled him to buy back the Thornhill estate in about 1725, where he built the present house to, it is thought, his own design. He died there in 1734 and is buried in Stalbridge Church.

Improvements to the land and farming methods in the Blackmore Vale developed in the eighteenth century, but the accelerated enclosure of common and downland caused bitter poverty among ordinary people and the ruin of many independent smallholders.

On one such smallholding that most remarkable and talented man William Barnes was born in 1801 at Rushay on Bagber Common, about two miles from Sturminster Newton. His father's family had

Following enclosure, squatters and smallholders built cottages in the wide verges laid out to compensate farmers for their loss of grazing rights – as here near Poll Bridge, west of Bishop's Caundle.

The poet of the Blackmore Vale is undoubtedly William Barnes
(1801-1886), who was born at Bagber, just outside Sturminster Newton.
The painting is by John Thorne, and dates from about 1845.

lived and farmed for generations at Gillingham and East Stour, but
the affairs of his orphaned forebears had been badly managed. This
meant that Williams's father John (1763-1846) had only the tenancy
of the smallholding at Bagber. He supplemented his income by day
labouring for neighbouring farmers and landowners. Living on
Bagber Common was a considerable help to the family and the young
William became so instinctively aware of the advantages that when,
later, the Common was enclosed, he knew exactly what privations the
poor would suffer, and said so in *The Common A-Took In*:

And then, bezides the cow, why we do let
Our geese run out among the emmet hills;
An' then when we do pluck em, we do get
Vor zeale some veathers an' some quills;

An' then, when I ha' nothen else to do,
Why I can teake my hook an' gloves, an' goo
To cut a lot o' vuzz and briars
Vor heten ovens, or vor lighten viers.

The school Barnes attended at Sturminster, and Vine House where he worked as an engrossing clerk for Thomas Dashwood, are still there. The 'cloty' Stour beloved of Barnes in his childhood still grows golden water lilies, though the elms are long gone and the river is sadly in need of cleaning out.

Barnes left the Vale when he was eighteen. In his long life he became a schoolmaster, poet, philologist (who had grasped the essentials of seventy-two languages and dialects), social historian, archaeologist, artist, musician and eventually clergyman, while his love for his wife Julia remains one of Dorset's and the country's great love stories.

William Barnes had courted Julia Miles for some eight years before their marriage in 1827 and her death in 1852 left him desolate. His grief found expression in poetry written in the Dorset speech of his childhood and in one of his most moving poems, *The Wife A-Lost*, he casts himself as a poor Dorset labourer:

Since now bezide my dinner-bwoard
Your vaice do never sound
I'll eat the bit I can avword
A-vield upon the ground;
Below the darksome bough, my love,
Where you did never dine,
An' I don't grieve to miss ye now,
As I at hwome do pine.

Throughout all the changes of William Barnes's life and the honour and respect in which he came to be held, the Blackmore Vale held his heart. The dialect poet turned philologist lovingly cherished its speech, vividly portrayed its life and to his great delight was eventually able to buy two fields hear his birthplace.

Thomas Hardy is often described as the Dorset writer and poet but in the Blackmore Vale that honour belongs indisputably to William Barnes. Hardy did however live briefly in the Vale. Married in 1874, he and his first wife Emma came in 1876 to live at Riverside Villas, overlooking the River Stour in Sturminster Newton. Here Hardy wrote *The Return of The Native* and observed later that these were 'our happiest days'.

Riverside Villas, Sturminster Newton, the then newly-built semi-detached house overlooking the River Stour where Thomas Hardy (1840-1928) and his wife Emma first set up a proper home together. Hardy wrote *The Return of the Native* in the upstairs front room on the right.

In Barnes's and Hardy's lifetimes probably the greatest single influence for social change was the growth of the railways. Trains opened up huge tracts of a Blackmore Vale little changed physically since the Middle Ages. The Somerset and Dorset Railway was established in 1863 from north of Blandford to Cole (for Bruton), and in 1874 from Bath to Bournemouth, enabling poor working class families to glimpse the sea and farmers' sons to go to London for the first time in their lives.

The coming of the railway also improved the health of Vale dwellers by making remote places accessible. Whereas girls worked long hours at home as gloving outworkers, then married the young man next door who was probably a relation, now boys and girls found mates over a much wider area and physical and mental health improved. The beloved 'Slow and Doubtful' Railway was savagely uprooted in the 1960s, leaving just a scattering of industrial archaeology and some cycle paths, though a real working railway from Bristol to Weymouth still runs along the Vale's western boundary.

Shillingstone Station in 1904. The arrival of the railway in the Blackmore Vale, with the opening of the Salisbury and Exeter Railway in 1859 and the Somerset and Dorset Railway four years later, took milk from the Blackmore Vale's dairy farms to the towns, and helped the Vale get through the late nineteenth-century depression in farming.

Roads have been widened and straightened in many places and the Blackmore Vale has a good record of care for its footpaths, green lanes and bridleways, which will be a great help when we examine the landscape in detail. And we are further helped in our quest by the existence of some excellent guide books. The Royal Commission on Historical Monuments published its two part survey of 'Central Dorset' in 1970, and a single volume on the 'North' in 1972. They are accurate, thorough and extremely well-illustrated, with the pictures arranged methodically by subject. This is helpful, for the text is full of dense architectural information and detail about medieval earthworks and can sometimes seem a bit plodding. These volumes are available in most Dorset libraries or can be ordered.

Dorset's most famous guidebook is the *History and Antiquities of the County of Dorset* by the Reverend John Hutchins (1698-1773). A Dorset man, born at Bradford Peverell, he held various Dorset livings, living for the last thirty years at Wareham. The first edition of the book came out in 1774, the second from 1798 and the third from

A road-working gang at Holnest in the 1930s.
Road widening and tarring took place throughout the Blackmore Vale in
the 1930s, linking farms and hamlets.

1861–1874: this edition was corrected and 'improved' by several noteworthy antiquarians, which makes it very reliable. This edition was republished in 1973 in four absolutely massive volumes.

Hutchins was devoted to his studies, sometimes irritated when parish duties interrupted them and given to wry observation with (unintentional) humour, as when he commented of William Freke of Hinton St. Mary who published a *Dictionary of Dreams* and died in 1744, 'His understanding was deranged but he acted as a Justice of the Peace for many years'.

My personal favourite of the classic Dorset guidebooks is *Highways and Byways in Dorset* (1906) by Frederick, later Sir Frederick Treves. This remarkable man, pupil of William Barnes, rescuer of the Elephant Man, surgeon to King Edward VII, informs his prose with sharp observation, scathing criticism, and above all with an abiding love for his county. Detail of books for further reading are listed at the end of this book.

EASTWARDS FROM THE CAPITAL

You can reach Sturminster Newton by either country lanes or broadish metalled highways. If you come from Blandford or Sherborne on the A357 you will reach the Newton half of the town with its fascinating mixture of timber-framed, brick and thatched houses and the remains of a 'Castle'. This once Iron Age fort became a Saxon manor (King Alfred bequeathed it to his son Ethelwold), and was later acquired by Glastonbury Abbey. Little remains of it now but the original Castle must have commanded an excellent view of the River Stour. The river here is wide and beautiful and the Mill beside it (manned and open to visitors) is well worth a visit.

In Newton too, as you come up the road from the Mill, turn right, and on your right you will see a sign saying 'Halter Path to Stalbridge'. Here five miles of cool, shaded walk along this ancient

The remains of the manor house which stand near the site of Sturminster Newton Castle. Shortly after the Dissolution of the Monasteries the manor of Sturminster was granted to Queen Katherine Parr, who built a manor house in the castle grounds.

Bagber Manor Farm was where my father was born. This photograph was taken by William Barnes' son in 1883, when the two of them revisited the scenes of Barnes's childhood. Barnes cherished the photograph, calling it the 'Haunted House'.

path will bring you to Bagber Manor Farm, as it was called when my father was born there, though it is now called Bagber Manor. This house was photographed in 1883 by the Revd. William Miles Barnes, the poet's eldest son, when he took his father on a visit to the scenes of his childhood.

Six year later the house was rebuilt by the Stalbridge Estate following a fire and became, my relations who lived there claimed, 'all windows'. There is a nod to the past though. It has a stone achievement-of-arms and a date stone of 1599 preserved on the front from the earlier house.

The Sturminster part, reached over a lovely six-arched stone bridge, is a town planner's hallucination, with the stump of the market cross, assorted shops tossed about the Market Place and narrow streets and lanes. The Cross was originally shaped like a perfectly formed fully ripe mushroom but one night in 1540 it was smashed to pieces by thieves hoping to find hidden gems.

There is much for the enthusiastic traveller to explore, from the old Union Workhouse Chapel (now the Museum) on the Bath Road and the Recreation Ground, in a lovely open position towards the River

Part of Sturminster Newton's charm is its mixture of building styles and periods. This view of Church Street includes a row of seventeenth or eighteenth century thatched brick-built cottages

Stour, to venerable Church Street and Tanyard Lane full of interesting houses of various ages. Tanyard Lane is a fascinating jumble of house shapes and styles and Church Street is bright with window boxes and colourful ceramic house signs.

The parish church was greatly extended in 1827 by the vicar, T.H. Lane Fox, a wealthy, energetic man who lavished a good deal of his own fortune on the church. William Barnes and his father had attended church faithfully and the church organist of that time, Tom Spinney, gave the young Barnes his first violin and singing lessons. Lane Fox became vicar after Barnes had left Sturminster but there was much goodwill between the two men and Barnes always referred to him as 'the good clergyman', so it is especially fitting that the beautiful oak lectern in the church is a tribute to William Barnes's memory.

Various tablets in the church testify to the charitable nature of the town's earlier inhabitants and offer a good insight into Victorian Sturminster. Money is left to 'young persons who do not receive parish relief', to 'large, indigent and industrious families' and of course apprentices. The eight stained glass windows are well-documented and repay study. Two of them are by a woman, Mary

A detail from the stained glass 'Arts and Crafts' style 'Resurrection' window in St Mary's Church, Sturminster Newton, by Mary Lowndes, a lifelong feminist and Britain's first woman stained glass maker, in memory of her father, vicar of Sturminster Newton for 36 years.

Lowndes (1857-1927), Britain's first woman stained glass artist.

There was a serious fire in the centre of the town in 1729 but parts of some of the fifteenth and sixteenth century houses there have survived. The White Hart and Swan Inns in the market place certainly convey an atmosphere of old commerce.

Sturminster was once famous for button and candle making and the manufacture of a woollen cloth called swanskin. From 1100, a market flourished there. This market, especially for cattle, brought great wealth to the town. The prosperity of Sturminster Newton was

The milk receiving platform of the Sturminster Newton & District
Farmers in the 1920s. Much of the milk was turned into cheese
and sent by rail to London.

My grandfather's cheese room at Cook's Farm,
just outside Stalbridge, in the 1890s.

always linked to dairy farming but the development of the railway
through the Blackmore Vale greatly increased this. Milk did not keep
so cheese was made on the farm premises. When landowners built or
rebuilt farm houses they often included a purpose built cheeseroom
where cheesemaking could be developed seriously (my grandfather at
Cook's Farm, Stalbridge, in the 1890's, developed cheese with celery
seeds in it, a real innovation).

The finished cheese was sold or auctioned at the market, but the development of the railway meant that fresh milk could be sold far afield by the producer. The market and the railway together brought great economic prosperity to Sturminster Newton.

Local people though still recall one terrible time in the 1930's when a calf was sent to market and found to be suffering from foot and mouth disease. This terribly contagious disease can still only be contained by the wholesale slaughter of animals that might have been infected and the entire stock of the cattle market had to be shot and burned. It was a dreadful time. The stench of burnt flesh and smoke drifted across the Vale for days – my own parents never forgot it.

The market was run for many years by a firm of auctioneers named Senior and Godwin with branches at Blandford, Sherborne and Gillingham. Sturminster Newton market closed in 1997. Its closure is greatly lamented still.

From Sturminster Newton it is less than a mile to Fiddleford Manor House, whose great hall and solar are thought to have been built for William Latimer, Sheriff of Dorset, in the late fourteenth century. The windbraces in the roof are unusual and lovely and the

Fiddleford Manor House. The fourteenth century building enjoys a lovely riverside settings and probably gives the best feel of what a medieval house was like of any in Dorset.

Looking up at the arched timber braces of the Solar in Fiddleford Manor House prior to its restoration.

building is open to the public. The whole area, the rest of the building (not open), the cottages, lane, Mill and stretch of river are beautiful and must not on any account be missed.

Manston and The Orchards (East Orchard and West Orchard) with fields of green grass and dairy cows still, are in the floor of the Blackmore Vale. Manston House was destroyed by fire in 1857 though some of the seventeenth century house survives, notably a large fireplace in the kitchen. A mausoleum was added when the house was rebuilt and some years later the then owner, Captain Hanham, erected a private crematorium there. This was in 1882. He cremated two of his relatives (on their instructions) and was himself cremated there a year later.

However, the practice of cremation had been given up in Saxon times and everyone had to be buried (for many years using woollen shrouds to help the woollen trade). The first public crematorium did not open until 1885, so Captain Hanham would seem to have been in advance of his time.

On the Manston to Child Okeford road one suddenly comes upon Fontmell Parva House, an elaborate looking red brick mansion whose central block dates from the Restoration and was built by

Fontmell Parva House, showing the original east front of about 1665 built by Admiral St Loe, and a fine example of Restoration architecture.

Admiral St. Loe, who brought back the mahogany panelling from Honduras. The drive though is a sea of aconites and snowdrops in early spring.

Hammoon takes its name from Ham (or home) of the Mohuns a great Norman family named de Mohun or Moyon. This family was

Okeford Fitzpaine

Manor Farm, Hammoon, showing the porch of about 1600. The tiny
village of Hammoon, meaning 'river-land of the Mohuns', lies beside the
River Stour and owes its name to the de Mohuns, who came from
Normandy with William the Conqueror.

first established in Dunster, Somerset, but by the time of the
Domesday Survey had become owners of a number of Dorset
manors, of which Hammoon was one.

The medieval village church has as its companion the Manor
House (long ago become the Manor Farm). Its roof is thatched and
Arthur Oswald in his 1935 classic *Country Houses of Dorset* calls it
a 'cottage manor house with only its classic porch and two storied
bay to the right to show that it was once a place of some account.'

A clutch of Okefords, Okeford Fitzpaine, Child Okeford and
Shilling Okeford (which you will find marked on the map as
Shillingstone) draw their names from many sources. The 'Okeford'
comes from a ford across the River Stour, perhaps marked by oak
trees. Okeford Fitzpaine takes its from a great family named
Fitzpaine, one of whose sons, Robert, stole King Henry III's seal, then
used it to manufacture indulgences exempting him from paying
certain dues on the estate.

The village is invariably described as 'pretty', which might make
one anxious, but it really is attractive, especially near the church, with

A detail from Isaac Taylor's 1765 map of Dorset. In the bottom right a line of tents is marked 'Camp in 1756'. It was here that General James Wolfe trained for climbing the Heights of Abraham by practising at Hambledon Hill (top left). Three years later Wolfe's foresight paid off when he captured Quebec from the French – though he lost his life in the process.

thatched and half-timbered and brick cottages. Any tendency to pretentiousness is kept in check by the local name for it of Ockford or Fippenny Ockford, and some newish houses are named 'Fippenny Hollow'.

Child Okeford takes its name possibly from 'chill' or from a 'Child' or knight who must once have lived there – we do not know who he was. The village lies in the lovely shadow of the great Iron Age hillfort on Hambledon Hill, with its huge, old yew wood at one end. Here the Clubmen, men who did not support King or Parliament but just wanted to live their lives in peace, demonstrated against the depredations of the Civil War, and here General Wolfe trained his men so efficiently that they were later able to scale the Heights of Abraham in Quebec.

Above Shillingstone maypole, which stood near the cross and is mentioned by Frederick Treves as still standing in 1906.

Above right Shillingstone Cross in about 1913. 'It stands in the roadway,' wrote Treves, 'a delicate Gothic pinnacle, with an orchard and a thatched cottage for a background'.

Ridgeway Lane is part of a Ridgeway of prehistory, a lovely, rutted, shaded lane where a lane leading from it has a beautifully (and expertly) laid hedge, now growing up well. The fields beside Ridgeway Lane, with the shape of great Hambledon beyond, have always seemed to me to exercise an unusually calming effect.

In Child Okeford a sixteenth-century rector composed 'The Old Hundredth' ('All People that on Earth do Dwell') though his church must have looked very different then. The tower of big greensand blocks remains but the rest is Victorian.

Shillingstone gets its name from the Eschellings, a family settled there of whom one, a wife named Alice, in the time of King John, paid that unreliable king protection money 'that her lord, John Eschellings, might not pass over the sea with horses and arms'. From 'Shellings Town' we soon get Shillingstone.

The village is remarkable for many things. The oak pulpit in the church was given by William Keen, a London merchant who came there in 1666 to escape the plague, in gratitude for having done so. In the first six months of the First World War this village of 543 souls sent a record 90 men to war, earning it the title of 'England's Bravest Village'.

Shillingstone kept its maypole for centuries after Cromwell (no mean achievement), William Barnes and Frederick Treves refer to it. There is also an old, well-restored, village cross which Treves describes as 'beautiful and graceful'.

Iwerne Courtney church is famous for the imprisonment of the Clubmen during the Civil War. They were so called either because they armed themselves with clubs or because they tried to form a club or association. They did this after having their corn trampled, their barns pillaged and their horses stolen by gangs of armed men supporting either the King or Parliament – the Clubmen did not care which.

Led by the rector of Compton Abbas, they rallied some five thousand men and, after skirmishes round about, two thousand of them gathered on Hambledon Hill to make a last stand. Cromwell himself described to General Fairfax how attempts were made to negotiate with them. These failed, the Clubmen were attacked by dragoons and the 300 prisoners taken in that day were imprisoned for the night in Shroton (Iwerne Courtney) Church. After this they – not surprisingly – promised to be dutiful in future and not come out again.

Iwerne Courtney and Iwerne Minster take their names from the River Iwerne, a little river which joins the larger Stour. Local people call Iwerne Courtney 'Shroton' from Sheriff's Town. There was a famous 'best frocks and bonnets' autumn fair held there for many years but it has ended now. William Barnes recaptures the breathless excitement of that event in his poem *Shroton Fair* when Poll and Nan rush upstairs:

To shift their things, as wild as heares;
An' pull'd out each o'm vrom her box
Their snow-white leace and newest frocks.

Shroton House and nearby Ranston are both now chiefly eighteenth century. Shroton House, two-storied and brick, though largely rendered now, dates from the first half of the eighteenth century. Inside there is eighteenth century pine panelling in two heights and the original oak staircase. Ranston House retains a

Clayesmore School, originally built in 1878 for the banker Lord Wolverton.

scrolled wrought-iron weathervane dated 1653 and its graceful eighteenth century west front, but there has been much rebuilding and some demolition since then.

Iwerne Minster Church has a stone steeple, rare in Dorset, and buried there is one John Willis who died in 1760. He was a writing master, not a highly regarded person in those days (Jane Austen's Emma is told by Mr. Knightly that if Harriet does not marry Robert Martin, she might eventually be glad to catch at the old writing master's son). This writing master, however, taught copper plate for thirty years at his school. His fame brought him pupils from all over the country and he died possessed of a considerable fortune.

There is a great house at Iwerne Minster, a Victorian mansion now become Clayesmore School. It was built in 1878 for Lord Wolverton to a design by Alfred Waterhouse, architect of the Natural History Museum in London. 'It is,' proclaims *Mates' Illustrated Guide to Dorsetshire* in 1900, 'a Perpendicular Gothic building of bold design'. In 1878, of course, it would be. However, the guide adds charitably, 'Nowhere are the poor more comfortably or healthily housed than in the Wolverton cottages'.

In 1908 the estate was bought by James Ismay, the wealthy son of the founder of the White Star Shipping Company (owners of the ill-fated *Titanic*), who gave the village a 'model village' air. He had a

Iwerne Minster. The village pump and – in the background – the stone shelter with its notice boards. The shelter was designed by Sir Giles Gilbert Scott, architect of Bankside Power Station (now Tate Modern), and was known as the 'War Office' – 'on the walls of which are pinned up the news of the day as cut from the morning papers . . . the outcome of a custom observed during the war [1914-18] when the important news of the day was posted on the village pump.'

liking for diamond-paned windows and half-timbering in houses of quiet red brick, designed hand-painted signs for the village shops and clothes for the village children. He also provided a village hall, complete with a miniature rifle range (now a private house), a village pump with a stone trough and a roof over it, and a stone shelter containing notice boards. Here the inhabitants can read local news and stay dry, a facility said to have been much appreciated in the First World War.

The estate was put up for sale in 1929 and became Clayesmore School, a flourishing public school for boys, and now girls. In recent years it has featured on television in an episode of 'Only Fools and Horses' involving a chandelier, and as a military academy in a film.

The interior of St Bartholomew, Sutton Waldron, which has now been completely restored and whose painted decorations and rich colours make it one of the loveliest of Victorian churches.

Sutton Waldron's Church of St. Bartholomew is one of the most attractive churches I know. Everything about it is attractive – its situation on a knoll, its old graveyard (now a nature reserve complete with a rustic seat), and its roof with neat banding in patterned and straight tiles. And there are many fully-grown trees, including – to quote from the old folk song – 'the oak and the ash and the bonny ivy tree' – though the ivy is so bonny here it could harm the others.

The church is Victorian but thank goodness only just – 1847. It was built by the rector Canon, later Archdeacon, Anthony Huxtable a scientific farmer sometimes considered to have pioneered the organic movement. His wife was immensely wealthy so he used her fortune to build the church, as one could in those days. The old Saxon church was demolished and this one erected with pale restrained stained glass, deep blue and red colour in the chancel arch with pale and dark blue bands of colour above. More colour shimmers in the ten Commandments and texts that abound, the walls are stencilled with coloured patterns and the chancel walls are painted in vibrant deep madder pink. The tiles are by Pugin and the painted decorations the work of Owen Jones, an influential architect and colour theorist. The decorations are thought to be the only remaining examples of his work in the United Kingdom. John Betjeman called it one of the loveliest examples of Victorian architecture and he was right. Don't miss it.

Fontmell Down gives a wonderful view across the Blackmore Vale, while Melbury Beacon gets its name from a bonfire being built there to warn of invasion by the Spanish Armada in 1588. It was not necessary to light it then, but it was lit, along with a chain of beacons around the Blackmore Vale, in 1988, to commemorate the three hundredth anniversary of the Spaniards' failure.

An attractive village, Fontmell Magna was the home of Philip Salkeld, the rector's son who, in 1857, won the Victoria Cross at the Siege of Delhi during the Indian Mutiny. Another son of Fontmell, Newman Flower, (1879–1964) born at the brewery and later a famous publisher, whose authors included Thomas Hardy, Winston Churchill and H.G. Wells, remembers going out ferreting with another boy. They both marvelled at the bullet holes put through the tail of the cock on top of the village maypole by the young Salkeld.

In the centre of the village there had been for generations an old

The memorial cross to Lieutenant Philip Salkeld VC,
the son of the rector, in Fontmell Magna churchyard.

The Crown Brewery, Fontmell Magna, with the brewer's house on the left.

elm, a gossip tree. It must have been a greatly valued amenity, for Newman Flower relates how isolated the village was in his youth. His father's salesmen were sometimes held up by highwaymen and none of the household was allowed out after dark. The tree had to be felled in 1976 but the lime tree that replaced it still flourishes.

Compton Abbas (once held by Shaftesbury Abbey) has a small airfield for light aircraft from where it is possible to take aeroplane trips out over the Vale. Many of the thatched farm houses and cottages in the village below are of seventeenth and eighteenth century origin and Crocker's Farm has the date 1660 incised above the west doorway and some windows.

The church is Victorian (1866), well built and lovingly cared for today by a small but devoted band of worshippers with a talent for tapestry, woodwork and bell-ringing. The old church, lower down the village, fell down in 1866, all except the tower. I find these remains very moving. There are the yew trees, gate and church path of old, the outline of the original church is plain and the tower firmly stands, yet some of the grave stones are dated 1865 and 1866. These worshippers were obviously interred just before the building collapsed. Among them still, as if keeping watch, are some huge mossy steps and stones, the remains of an old preaching cross.

GILLINGHAM AND BEYOND

You will perhaps remember that I proposed skirting lightly around Shaftesbury on the south side. I have nothing against Shaftesbury. It is a lovely old town, full of history and Abbey ruins, the famous Gold Hill of the old Hovis advertisements and wonderful views over the Vale. It simply does not fall within my map of the Blackmore Vale, so I intend going straight to Motcombe. Treves says of Motcombe that 'in the spring the little place is as full of white blossoms as is a temple cloister in Japan'. Motcombe is a very different temple cloister nowadays. It is the home of the splendid Shaftesbury and Gillingham Show, full of fat sheep, wonderful local food, crafts, children's art, rabbits and hens.

Gillingham was once densely afforested. In 1210 King John rewarded two huntsmen for killing wolves there. Half a mile from the town a palace built by a Saxon or Norman king became the Sandringham and Balmoral of the early medieval period, for King Henry I, John, Henry III and Edward I stayed there. Henry III, an enthusiastic connoisseur of fine buildings who appreciated comfort in his palaces, particularly appreciated the King's Court. He had a chapel built over the royal chamber (panelled with oak of course), a chapel for Queen Eleanor and a new kitchen with a round opening for the smoke from roasting venison.

The King's Court was deep in the Forest of Gillingham so that it was an easy matter for Henry III or his bailiff to order the felling of forty great oaks at a time for building work. Gillingham oaks were sent to Sherborne Castle, Corfe and the Friars' Preaching building at Gloucester and the medieval forest hummed with activity.

Sadly, however, Edward I had neither the time nor inclination to visit the palace much. His last visit was in the spring of 1278 and gradually the place fell into ruin until only the foundations were left. In the eighteenth century these too were plundered to repair the road

Gillingham Bridge, Dorset by John Constable. The painting, which is in Tate Britain, dates from the wet August of 1823 when Constable was staying with his close friend, Archdeacon John Fisher, the vicar of Gillingham. One of Fisher's children recalled Constable sitting with his easel at the right-hand corner of the picture.

to Shaftesbury. All that remains now is a green space called King's Court. The forest was cleared by Charles I to accommodate the wishes of his old tutor Sir James Fullerton, to whom he had leased it, to the great annoyance of local people whose riots had to be put down by the military.

The Town Bridge over the Stour was painted by John Constable in 1823. The town used to be known for silk throwing, breweries, bricks of a particularly raw vermilion and still much in evidence, bacon curing and a bone factory. For years, this latter caused a throat gripping stench by boiling bones to make glue.

Its famous Free School, later Grammar School, was founded before 1516, the exact date is not known. It was designed among other things for the instruction of youth in good literature. Hutchins tells us that 'in the great rebellion' (the Civil War) 'it was full of the sons of loyal gentleman'. Lord Clarendon (Charles II's Chancellor) had part of his education here. Clarendon's daughter Anne Hyde became pregnant by the future King James II in 1660, to her father's dismay. James married Anne and she became the mother of Queens Mary and

The magnificent memorial to Sir Hugh Wyndham (1603-1684)
in St. Nicholas Church, Silton, flanked by his two weeping daughters,
Blanch and Rachell, representing two forms of grief.

Anne. Gillingham's old Grammar School was one of the first in the area to become a comprehensive school.

In place of the old industries, Gillingham, well-situated on the railway's London line, is set to become the new Swindon. Building works are everywhere, savagely eating into the rich farming lands of the Vale and mosaic of old hedges that are all that remain of the Royal Forest. The River Stour at Milton-on-Stour is just a stream a few miles from its source. The mill once called Parhams, but now Purnes Mill, was also painted by Constable who often stayed with his friend John Fisher, the Vicar of Gillingham. Milton church has a graceful spire (unusual in the Blackmore Vale).

Quite different is the remote little church of Saint Nicholas at

Silton which is well worth a visit for its extreme contrasts. Parts of the building are late twelfth century but the walls were stencilled throughout in 1870 to designs by Clayton and Bell, well-known ecclesiastical designers, Alfred Bell having been born in Silton. Also to be found in this isolated medieval church is a huge grey and white marble monument with barley sugar twist columns. It was erected in 1692, eight years after his death, to Sir Hugh Wyndham, Justice of the Court of Common Pleas for thirteen years in the time of the Commonwealth and under King Charles II. It really is vast. Judge Wyndham stands beneath a highly decorated stone proscenium arch. He is flanked by two mourning women, with skull and hourglass, who are weeping with a verve and theatricality that would never have been tolerated in the eighteenth century.

Silton Church is also remarkable for its independence. In 1972 it took such a determined stand against amalgamation with neighbouring parishes that it has remained independent ever since. Its services are entirely according to the Book of Common Prayer, with refugees from modern liturgies increasing its already large congregation.

We leave Silton church and its splendid backdrop of the downs, for Bourton, an area once well-known for flax growing and linen

The tiny church at Langham, built in 1921 as a memorial to the men of the hamlet and local estate who were killed during the First World War.

Looking west from Kington Magna churchyard. The view is magnificent, encompassing Henstridge, Stalbridge, and the flat low-lying valley of the River Cale (which joins the Stour near Marnhull).

weaving. In 1992 a bypass was hefted across the north of Silton and to the south of Bourton, revealing the skeleton of an Jurassic Age Ichthyosour and evidence of a little wayside smithy. Bourton, on the borders of Dorset, Wiltshire and Somerset is now, with the London/Exeter traffic diverted, much quieter.

Between Buckhorn Weston and Gillingham stands Langham with early medieval settlement remains and, since 1921, a tiny thatched church built as a memorial to the men of the hamlet and estate who died in the First World War. It is designed in simple Arts and Craft Gothic and services are still held there, notably at Harvest Festivals but, be warned, all the lanes around look alike and the tiny place is difficult to find (*for illustration see previous page*).

Buckhorn Weston is near a rather splendid railway tunnel in which trains have always put on a great burst of speed when going towards Templecombe. In the days of steam they chuffed sedately along until they entered the tunnel, revved up and emerged from it at top speed and with ear splitting shrieks. They still belt out of the tunnel, but more calmly. It is also a parish that boasts the extraordinarily named Caggypole Farm and an inn with an eighteenth century coach house

After the harvest. A distant view of Stour Provost from near Fifehead Magdalen, with Duncliffe Hill in the background.

now incorporated in the dwelling, with traces in the walls of former coach house doorways.

Kington Magna is divided by the little River Cale into two parts – Kington and Nyland. Nyland is surrounded by marshland while the Kington Magna part stands on rising ground. The position of the churchyard is especially lovely and Treves says firmly that the village 'commands one of the most beautiful views of the famous Vale'. Monica Hutchings in her 1965 book *Inside Dorset* says of Kington Magna that 'it looks as if the Upper Valley of the Stour was about to fall upon the Vale'. You may make your own mind up, of course, but this view is not to be missed. The church was rebuilt in the 1860's except for the fine fifteenth century tower. As well as a coat-of-arms of Charles I, the church has an unusual carved stone reredos and light flagstones on the floor of the nave with slate insertions among them,

'The slowly meandering River Stour, the true source of the Blackmore Vale's richness', seen here at Trill Bridge between Stour Provost and Fifehead Magdalen.

like paths. A medieval fishpond can be seen immediately below the church and there are well-marked footpaths in the steeply sloping fields around it.

The road from Kington Magna slopes steeply down towards the A30 and Fifehead Magdalen but take this slowly, stopping from time to time, for the views to the right across the Vale, glimpsed through the hedge to the right are lovely. Monica Hutchings says of Fifehead Magdalen, 'This area is neither truly vale nor downland – a shelf between the upper and lower valleys which the Stour had to make for itself when deflected by the mass of Duncliffe.'

The village straddles a limestone ridge overlooking the Stour and River Cale, which join among the Oxford Clay meadows that surround it. Like all Dorset's 'Fifeheads' it owes its name to its being assessed at five hides at Domesday, a hide originally being the amount of land required to support a family and its dependents.

A pleasing assembly of sixteenth and seventeenth century farmhouses and cottages is to be found in this little place, and a parliament of 'glossy preoccupied rooks in their swaying attics' creates merry bedlam outside the church, while in spring the ground around it is strewn with snowdrops and daffodils.

STALBRIDGE AND
THE CAUNDLES

The busy A30 runs through West Stour but to reach it from Fifehead Magdalen you may be lucky enough to find an unspoiled lane. These abound in this area, sometimes marked 'To Farms Only' or the name of a farm, but more often not marked with anything at all, so that you will suddenly come upon a scene out of a Constable painting or a group of oak trees descended from the Forest of Gillingham. Fields in this well-watered stretch of country tend to be small still, though not the little paddocks they used to be. Old Duncliffe Hill stands like a rounded sentinel and the villages have similar looking churches with squat, typically Dorset towers.

West Stour, mentioned in the Domesday Survey, has some attractive farm houses and cottages, including Manor Farm House covered with stone slates and dating from about 1800. Buildings of another kind arose there in 1988 when brick foundations for six dwellings appeared on a caravan site, followed by tiling. The local Council and two inspectors ruled that these 'permohomes' – structures which could not be moved in any practicable way – were not caravans. The Environment Secretary of the day, however, permitted them and West Stour received unusual media coverage of the event.

East Stour, another of the Stour holdings of Domesday, has nearby wooded Duncliffe for company. This famous landmark in the Vale was once owned by the Forestry Commission who planted it with conifers, so that it looked for years like a black hill. Later it had the great good fortune to be bought by the Woodland Trust which means that trees are being thinned and light let into this ancient woodland again. Visitors are encouraged now and guided walks arranged.

The old church at East Stour was demolished and a new one built

The tenth century Saxon cross shaft at East Stour is
richly decorated in plants and interlace patterns.

in 1842, though some fittings from the old one were installed.
However, in 1939 during the demolition of a house, a fragment of a
cross shaft was discovered. A square stone column 2 feet 4 inches
high, it was richly decorated with Saxon vine scroll work and dated
from the late tenth or early eleventh centuries.

East Stour is also remarkable for the house where Henry Fielding,
the author of *Tom Jones* lived. The old rectory in which he wrote the
novel has been demolished, but Church Farm stands on the site. He
spent the early years of his marriage there riotously getting through a
fortune, mostly his wife's. She was a Salisbury beauty and said to be
the model for Sophia Weston, the novel's heroine, though another
view asserts that the heroine was Betty Weston who lived at Gants

Mill, Bruton, and was painted by Hogarth.

Nearby Stour Hill gives superb views of the Blackmore Vale, Somerset and the downs beyond Mere. Stour Provost has a still existing pattern of long narrow fields showing that at one time open fields lay around it. In this area, notably at Stour Row, the verges of the lanes were broad so from the eighteenth century small cottages were built on them. It often happened in the Blackmore Vale that when fields were enclosed extra large verges were laid beside the roads in an attempt to compensate cottagers for the grazing rights they had lost.

Many farm houses and cottages at Stour Provost and Stour Row are old and attractive to look at. Church House, some fifty yards west of the church, has oak panelling in the parlour, and Diamond Farm, 165 yards south-west of the church, has a through passage flanked by plank-and-muntin partitions in which the top rails and the edges of each of the vertical muntins are moulded. Both houses are early seventeenth century.

Stour Row has a number of well-documented cottages with slate covered or thatched roofs and five seventeenth or early eighteenth century farmhouses near its eastern boundary. One of these, Jolliffe's Farm, still retains its original plank-and-muntin partitions upstairs and down.

The Church of St. Andrew at Todber was in ruins in the mid

An engraving by William Barnes of Church Farm,
East Stour, which stands on the site of the rectory in which
Henry Fielding (1705-1754) wrote *Tom Jones*.

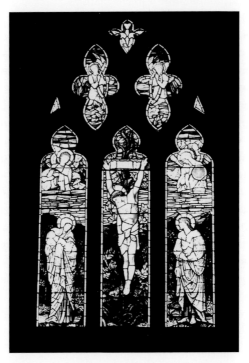

Marnhull Church. The 'Crucifixion' east window (1881)
by Edward Burne Jones, commissioned as a memorial to
Robert Kennard, the son of the rector.

nineteenth century (it is amazing how many were at that time) so the
Marchioness of Westminster rebuilt it at her own expense. In the
course of the rebuilding several large fragments of a Saxon stone cross
were found. It has been reassembled and is now in the church. Todber
stone, an attractive creamy stone from local quarries has been much
used here.

Hinton St. Mary, an attractive village, especially off the main
Sturminster Newton road, has a seventeenth century Manor House
and a lovely old tithe barn now converted into an theatre. Cutt Mill
on the road to Marnhull, just below the Old Post Office on the left,
is down an unmarked lane. The first scene that meets the eye is a coal
yard, but carry on down to the River Stour and the beautiful Cutt
Mill with its old mill pool. The river here is fringed with bulrushes

and shaded by oaks. Deer come out of the woods to graze and in the water are the yellow clotes so beloved of William Barnes, whose 'Pentridge By The River' stands nearby. It is important to concentrate on the natural beauty of this spot for the river is in need of cleaning out and the old mill building was recently burnt down.

In modern times Hinton St. Mary's most remarkable claim to national fame has been the discovery of the Roman mosaic with the head of Christ described earlier. We now take quiet roads (unless you are unlucky) to the big scattered village of Marnhull, said to be the second largest village in the country.

Marnhull has been famous for many things – most unusually perhaps, according to one eighteenth century rector, for being remarkable for tall people, both men and women. Its manor, named Nash Court, was given in 1544 by Henry VIII to Catherine Parr, the queen who survived him, though there is no evidence that she ever visited it. From her it passed to Edward VI, then to Elizabeth I. It has been a place where adherents of the old Catholic religion have lived since 1651 when a Roman Catholic family named Hussey bought Nash Court. And of course, in the nineteenth century as 'Marlott', Marnhull became the home of Hardy's doomed Tess of the D'Urbervilles. The Crown Inn, called by Hardy 'The Pure Drop Inn' when Jack Durbeyfield first learned of his family's former greatness, still has a 'Pure Drop' bar.

Marnhull is an extraordinarily well-documented village. In 1931 the Womens's Institute won first prize for their best village history in a country competition. This was published and used by the Marnhull Festival of Britain Committee as a basis for their extremely ambitious history, *The Marn'll Book*, published in 1952 with many good illustrations and detailed accounts of every aspect of village life.

The earliest architectural remains of the church are Norman – a pillar with grotesque heads carved on it. Marnhull has traditionally been considered a prosperous place and as long ago as the reign of King John the church was big enough to have a chancel, nave and north aisle. Parish registers and church accounts are well preserved as are accounts of the oppressive exactions for labour and services of successive Abbots of Glastonbury upon Marnhull people. One record, which has now disappeared but was quoted by Treves, is the splendid epitaph of a rector to his clerk John Warren who died in 1752 aged 94, and his wife:

Here under this stone
Lie Ruth and old John
Who smoked all his life
And so did his wife.
And now there's no doubt
But their pipes are both out
Be it said without joke
That life is but smoke
Though you live to fourscore
'Tis a wiff and no more.

There are many interesting old houses and farm houses to admire in Marnhull. The old rectory has a lovely eighteenth century front door, though the cellars are said to date from the fourteenth century. Pope's Farm, a neat, stout, stone-mullioned house on the Stalbridge road, also called Chantry Farm, dates from the early seventeenth century, though a building beside it has Tudor doorways. This building was, until the coming of paraffin lamps, a candle factory where small tallow candles called 'farthing dips' were made. The other candles made there were called 'rush lights' as they had a rush in the centre for a wick.

Seniors Farm, west of the church, dates from around 1500. It might once have been the residence of a well-endowed chantry priest or the grange of the Abbot. Many original features remain, notably a medieval window with original glass and the initials 'J. C.' which would have stood for John Chinnock, Abbot of Glastonbury who died in 1407. There is some superb fourteenth century panelling above the stairwell and some original painted decorations remain on the plank-and-muntin partition. Superimposed on the decoration of one plank of this is a painting of a crowned figure in an ermine edged yellow robe and holding a sword or sceptre. The figure is often thought to be that of Edward VI.

Leaving Marnhull on the Stalbridge and Lydlinch road means a steep descent into the Vale down Cox Hill. This is a wonderful hill to walk or better still cycle down in the early evening, when the Stour is

Two farmhouses built of local limestone from quarries near Marnhull. Seniors Farm (*left*) is just west of the church and dates from 1500, whilst Pope's Farm (*right*) is on the Stalbridge road.

a silver ribbon and the light is soft and gentle. Cycling down Cox Hill then is even more exciting if, whizzing down, you recite poetry very loud. Ernest Dowson's *Vesperal* sounds particularly lovely at such times:

'Strange grows the river on the sunless evenings,
The river comforts me, grown spectral, vague and dumb'.

If the river is in flood, and the mill pool at King's Mill greatly swollen, the resident swans have an extended playground. This road

The River Stour at King's Mill Bridge.

leads to Stalbridge, but let us first go straight on to Thornhill past the drive to Thornhill House and the Cleopatra's needle type obelisk marking the accession of King George II, to whose dynasty and reign the painter owed much. On the Sturminster side of the little hamlet of Lydlinch, the little Caundle Brook joins the River Lydden, near where the old humpbacked bridge, probably built in the 1830's, had to be supplemented in the Second World War. It became clear as the war progressed towards the Second Front that this bridge would not be able to bear heavy military traffic, so in 1942 Canadian Army engineers erected a Callender-Hamilton galvanised steel lattice girder bridge, heavier than a Bailey bridge. It is still in use, strengthened to take 40 ton lorries and decorated with flags on D-Day Anniversaries. Lydlinch has a venerable church dedicated to St. Thomas à Beckett and five bells admired by William Barnes:

'Vor Lydlinch bells be good vor sound
An' liked by all the naighbours round'

It has also, as you turn on to the Dorchester road, a venerable common – acres that have never been enclosed, where blackthorn flourishes and nightingales sing.

Stock (marked on the map as Stock Gaylard) has an immense park around it containing pure Menil Fallow deer. More spotted than common fallow deer, these do not produce twins and do not breed

Menil fallow deer in Stock Park, Stock Gaylard.

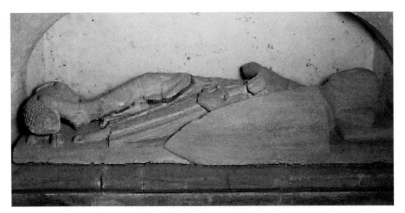

St Barnabas Church, Stock Gaylard, contains the fine stone effigy of Sir Ingelramus de Walys, who died fighting in Jerusalem during the Crusades. He is wearing chain mail, a shield hangs from one shoulder, his right hand holds the pommel of his sword, and his spurred feet rest on a lion.

with any others except fallow deer, which means that if wild deer penetrate Stock Park it will not dilute the strain.

The lovely little deer are a reliable weather vane. If they are beside the iron railings by the road, it will be wet. If they are right out across the park and can barely be glimpsed, it will be fine. The park and acres of the estate adjoining have for many years been the property of the Yeatman family so all the white farm gates are supported with a black Y in the middle. I have always found when driving from Dorchester towards Lydlinch with a car full of children that they enjoy being divided into two teams to see which can spot the most Y gates on the sides of the road.

The Queen Anne house visible from the road is not open to the public, but the little church has a service on the fifth Sunday. When it was restored in 1884 a skeleton and scraps of red leather were found under a stone effigy. Established as a Knight Templar who had died fighting in Jerusalem in 1274, his remains were reverently re-interred and the stone effigy remains a lovely sight.

If we now retrace our steps to Thornhill and turn left we come to Stalbridge where Charles I spent an October night in 1644 between the battles of Marston Moor and Naseby. He stayed in the old mansion in the Park (pulled down in 1822) where a few years later

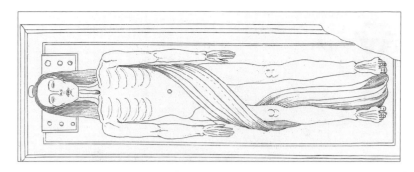

The drawing in Hutchins *History of Dorset* of the effigy of a corpse in one of the side chapels of the Church of St Mary, Stalbridge. The reality is even more gruesome and emaciated than in the drawing.

Robert Boyle made his famous experiments. When the common around the house was enclosed in the eighteenth century, five miles of dry stone wall were erected around the land which became Stalbridge Park.

The church once had a 'fayre chapell built by a Thornhull' an ancestor of the painter. It also had the tombstone in the nave of the last Abbot of Sherborne who, after the Dissolution of the Monasteries in the time of Henry VIII, ended his days as rector there. Sadly, the Victorian restorers attacked it with such zeal that the church is now rather full of pitch pine and lavatory tiles, the trademarks of those philistines. On a table tomb in a side chapel there is a cadaver effigy of a corpse in a shroud, said to be one of only three in the country.

'It is', says Treves, 'a gruesome object for the body of the unknown is so profoundly emaciated that the ribs appear as entrenchments through the skin' (Treves was a famous surgeon and it shows). The church clock had a carillon added in the 1890's which has recently been restored and now plays well-known hymn tunes melodiously every three hours in the daytime. The rector of the church from 1837-1867 was the Revd. L.C. Powys, grandfather of the writing Powyses.

Stalbridge High Street is an architectural delight. Coming from the church you pass Red Lion Court dating from about 1700, the former Red Lion Hotel and Inland Revenue office. The original mounting block is still there and some time later the building had a top storey added to make a ballroom. The Red Lion ballroom was the focus of

Stalbridge's 12 feet high market cross once stood in the centre of a huge medieval market place, and is the best preserved in Dorset. It is thought to have been commissioned by Galfridus de Mervin in gratitude for his having survived a battle against the Saracens in 1309. This engraving by William Barnes clearly shows the figure of Christ, with a lamb at his feet.

local social activity before the two wars and the two old tortoise stoves that warmed the dancers are still there.

The market cross in the High Street is the best of Dorset stone crosses. It was originally in the middle of the huge medieval market place and a plate on it describes it as 'fifteenth century'. Legend has it that it was first commissioned by Galfridus de Mervin who survived a battle against the Saracens in 1309, and there used to be a public house in Stalbridge called the Saracen's Head. Cromwell (somehow) missed the cross and now, encircled with hefty wooden posts by the local authority, it is hoped that modern traffic will miss it also.

I often think that Gold Street, Stalbridge, is architecturally the most interesting street in the Blackmore Vale, embracing everything from stone and thatch, in cottages like the one above, to substantial Georgian town houses and converted Regency shops.

Leland described the High Street as 'metely well builded'. Behind the Tudor extension to a house called Silk Hay on the corner of Silk House Barton (where fine silk stockings were made in the eighteenth century) a medieval hall house extends to the right across or behind three modern dwellings. The first retains its medieval front, the next has a late Victorian shop front and the fourth, now the newsagent, has an elegant eighteenth century addition. It is said, though not proved, that this hall house was the retirement home of the last Abbot of Sherborne, John Barnstable.

The name Stalbridge is said to derive from the Saxon 'Staplebreicg' or 'Staplebrige' (meaning a bridge over staples or piles) and Thomas Hardy's character in his story 'Squire Petrick's Lady' lived in Stalbridge in 'Stapleford Park'. However, the little town is some two miles from the River Stour, the bridge has not been identified and modern thinking inclines to the name being derived from 'Staple Ridge'. This place of Saxon origin was well settled into two separate parts – Stalbridge and Stalbridge Weston – by the time of the Domesday Survey. Then a series of farmsteads was carved out of the forest around Stalbridge in the thirteenth and fourteen centuries – farms with names like Gomershay, Hargrove and Cooks, which are still there and still isolated.

The landscape from Stalbridge to and around the Caundles villages is varied and interesting. Ralph Wightman, defining the shape of the land, explains that bands of rock such as Corallion or Corn Brash limestone are narrow, while the adjoining strips of Oxford Clay are much wider. These wide strips of clay dominate the farming, producing good grass and a plentiful water supply. If you dig a pit in the clay in the Vale it quickly becomes a pond and my own abiding childhood memory of my father's farm at Stalbridge is of the cows, stogged in mud, lumbering back to the yard for milking in deep muddy ruts exactly fitting their gait.

The name Caundle is amongst the most enigmatic of all Dorset place-names. Indeed it has been suggested that the Caundle villages get their name from the days of King Arthur and that 'Caundle' is the name that Romano-British tribesmen gave to the chain of hills dividing Dorset from Somerset.

Purse Caundle can be reached from Stalbridge by finding the Post Office in the High Street, going up Barrow Hill behind it and keeping on a picturesque little byway until you reach the road to Sherborne. Turn left, then left at the Purse Caundle sign. You soon see on your right the lovely Purse Caundle Manor House. King John, that passionate huntsman, gave the original manor house and land to the steward responsible for looking after his hounds taken sick or injured when hunting in the Blackmore Forest. The present manor house is fifteenth century, probably built in the reign of Edward IV and was built by one Richard Long, a member of a wealthy Wiltshire clothier family. It still retains its large open hall and 'from its gable end', says Arthur Oswald, waxing lyrical, 'there hangs out a medieval oriel, like a lantern to light passers by'. It really is a beautiful house and what appears to be a moat, or perhaps a brook, runs behind it. Passion flowers seem to grow well here and a few months ago I saw the front

Purse Caundle Manor House from the lane. King John gave the original manor house and land to the steward responsible for looking after hounds injured when the king 'coursed wild beasts in Blackmore' – the great Royal Forest that once included much of the Vale.

of a house opposite the manor house smothered with their blossoms.

Dr. Nathaniel Highmore is buried at Purse Caundle. His father was the rector there and the son, after studying at Oxford, practised at Sherborne. He was a physician and anatomist, a friend and close associate of the great William Hervey who discovered the circulation of the blood. Nathaniel Highmore became famous for his studies in anatomy and has given his name for all time to 'The antrum of Highmore', a cavity in the face. He died in 1685.

Stourton Caundle, once the home of the Stourton family, has some interesting houses and fine porches and especially farm buildings, with a good view from Haddon Lodge on Cockhill. A daughter of Haddon Lodge, Margaret Fernandes, married Wilfred Askwith, rector of Stalbridge in 1930 in the church here. The marriage is remembered still in the district for the rector was popular (he later became Bishop of Blackburn, then of Gloucester), and the bride's ultra-modern mid-calf dress with scalloped hem was quite lovely.

The Trooper Inn gets its name from a table being erected outside to enable young men to join the army in the war against Napoleon.

Flapper fashion in the Vale. The wedding of Margaret Fernandes and the rector of Stalbridge in Stourton Caundle Church in 1930.

The landscape of the Caundles is varied and interesting as Oxford Clay spills over a limestone ridge of Corn Brash. There used to be many common fields. In 1709 thirty five tenants farmed over 250 parcels of land, but by 1797, as a result of enclosures, nine tenants farmed 175. The fields around Stourton Caundle are flat and good for dairy farms, at least one of which has been farmed by the same family for six generations. As well as cows there has been a tradition around the Caundles of arable farming and cider making. Some of the apple orchards are gone now but cider was made at Brunsells Farm until within the last twenty years, where the cider house and press were still intact.

Old trees and quiet lanes, with high banks where eltrot flowers thickly in midsummer, are still to be found in the Caundle villages and wandering about in them one is all the time aware of the hills, of the chain of hills dividing Dorset from Somerset that gives the villages their name, and of gentle Bulbarrow to the South.

Bishop's Caundle was called Caudel Episcopi in the thirteenth century, the Bishop being the Bishop of Salisbury. There are some pleasant lanes leading to the village and the pub, The White Hart, has a large old stone mounting block in front. In the fields behind this pub Thomas Hardy's vision comes to life – his sense of the green sea of the Blackmore Vale washing up to the bare chalk uplands. The fields towards Bulbarrow are more rolling, making the light gleam softly and the hills look blue in the distance.

A bit further on lies Bishop's Down and then the last of the Caundles – Caundle Marsh. I was brought up to call this place Marsh Caundle with the distinguishing name first, but books about the Blackmore Vale call it Caundle Marsh. It is a small place, marshy no longer and with its own Victorian church.

We should not leave the whole area of Stalbridge and the villages and towns around it without being aware of the local Forest Marble stone. This stone has been quarried for the past millennia or more throughout the Blackmore Vale. Forest Marble beds of varying width were formed when the Blackmore Vale was a shallow primordial sea, some 160 million years ago. The stone can be split easily because the width varies and this means it has been used for buildings, roofing, dry-stone walling, paving, cobbles, flagstones and tiles, giving buildings a stout, weatherproof appearance. The broken edge of this stone is dark grey but from the ground it has a warm soft brown look on which the setting sun looks well.

St John's Almshouses near Sherborne Abbey, the dry-stone wall surrounding Stalbridge Park, the house named Silk Hay in Stalbridge High Street (where the half-hipped shape of the roof is a particular feature), the walls of Stourton Caundle Church, the roof of Purse Caundle Manor House, all these are of Forest Marble stone tiles, and because this excellent indigenous building material was so readily to hand, it explains why there are few timber-framed houses in the Blackmore Vale.

Sometimes, on for instance old farm houses, you will see just a frill of Forest Marble tiles around the edge, the rest being modern tiles. However, the 1947 Town and Country Planning Act and vigilant local authorities have done much to restrain this practice and the original Forest Marble quarry between Henstridge and Stalbridge is still in business.

THE WESTERN EDGE

We start our journey towards the western edge of the Blackmore Vale at the village of Longburton (one word on maps but sometimes written 'Long Burton', as if there were also a Short Burton. Perhaps there once was, for it is now a very long village). The last time I was there I made a foray into the church after hearing a talk about the Churchill's of Blenheim coming from the area. Sure enough, there was the evidence, a daughter of the Winston family commemorated here married John Churchill from nearby Glanville's Wootton. They became grandparents of the first Duke of Marlborough and ancestors of Sir Winston Churchill. There are other effigies here with them – all beautifully preserved.

Moving west to the hamlet of Lillington (which Treves calls

The tomb (1609) of Sir Thomas Winston and his wife Dionise in the Church of St James, Longburton. They were ancestors of the 1st Duke of Marlborough, passing on their surname to their most distinguished descendant, Sir Winston Churchill.

Lillington, showing the skilfully converted barn beside the church.

'Lillington the Obscure') we find the entirely Prayer Book church, which uses no modern liturgies, only the Book of Common Prayer, and a tithe barn dating from about 1600. This is now a private house and is quite the most skilful barn conversion I have seen. Lillington was once the seat of the Cole family, a member of whose family died in 1669 and, according to Hutchins, was awarded this epitaph:

> Reader you have within this grave
> A Cole rak'd up in dust,
> His courteous fate saw it was late
> And that to bed he must.
> Then do not doubt the Cole's not out
> Tho'it in ashes lie,
> The little spark, now in the dark,
> Will like the Phoenix rise.

Thornford village on a bank of the River Yeo is a request stop on the Bristol to Weymouth railway (as are Yetminster and Chetnole). This line, 'The Heart of Wessex Line', kept open in spite of many knavish tricks designed to close it in the 1970's, is now being

Thornford Bridge Halt in 1962, when it still retained the two staggered platforms either side of the bridge. Only one platform remains, and the station is now a request stop on the 'Heart of Wessex Line', kept open to encourage ramblers.

vigorously promoted. Parties of ramblers design their outings around the train stops and on Saturdays near Christmas you might meet Father Christmas.

The line was begun in 1845 and completed to Weymouth in 1857. Thornford was originally Thornford Bridge Halt and was only opened in 1936. It had two staggered wooden platforms and a pair of shelters lit by oil lamps. One of the advantages about the present 'Heart of Wessex' partnership between the railway and various local authorities is that packs of information about walks from it can be bought from South Somerset District Council's Offices at Churchfields, Wincanton, or by visiting www.heartofwessex.org.uk. Posters at each stopping place give useful information about the area and train times. But if you go to Thornford by train be warned, after walking up from the railway line to the road there is no sign indicating which way to go. You turn left.

A four-roomed Roman farmhouse with a tessellated pavement was uncovered, whilst the churchyard of the Church of St. Mary Magdalene, spacious and well kept, affords the most lovely views towards the north west and the Somerset borders.

The tithe tomb outside the Church of St Magdelene, Thornford. The small recess was where tenants once annually placed 5 shillings (25p) to prevent the lord of the manor taking tithes of hay.

In the churchyard to the right as you approach the porch is a tithe tomb. It has a small recess on the top and it is said that tenants placed five shillings in it to prevent the lord of the manor from taking tithes of hay during the year. In the church there is a wonderful little memorial in stained glass in the chancel to a Dr. Sparrow who was vicar of Sherborne in about 1419. It shows a sparrow pulling a harrow. The harrow is a sturdy oblong iron contraption, the sort routinely made by a medieval blacksmith, which the sparrow is pulling along effortlessly with one thin leg.

There are some fine seventeenth century farmhouses and farm buildings, notably old stalls and barns of working farms and Greenhill Farm has a lovely view of a green hill with, when I last saw it, a band of new, rich, brown ploughed land on the lower part of it – an arresting sight. Thatched houses abound, as well as porches, both rustic and iron-framed, and at The Old School I noticed some beautifully shaped clay tiles on the roof.

A stone clock tower, a large and rather ugly memorial to Queen Victoria's Diamond Jubilee, stands in a prominent position in the village. It has attempted to keep up with the times though, for a light was added to it to commemorate King George V's Silver Jubilee in 1935.

The houses and farm houses of Yetminster are a delight to the eye. It is probably unwise to arrive there by train as you have to walk up to the village along a pot-holed road with a view of warehouse type buildings quite unrelated to the landscape. However, some lovely stone mullion windowed old farm houses and the Old School (now a private house) complete with school bell, soon improve one's mood.

St. Andrew's Church has an old faceless clock that chimes the National Anthem some six times a day out over the graveyard. The graveyard displays a set of rules forbidding glass jars, oasis, wire, cellophane, paper or permanent plant-holders and asking for the removal of Christmas wreaths by the end of January. The rules are firmly kept, giving the churchyard a frozen, time-warped look.

Just beyond the church is a lovely old longhouse with a fifteenth century doorway and cusped windows, though the rest is older. This is Upbury Farm and here Benjamin Jesty (1736–1816) pioneered vaccination against smallpox. He had noticed that his milkmaids often caught cowpox from the cows and, if they did, they did not catch smallpox which was often fatal, so he developed a technique of

Upbury Farm, Yetminster. It was here that Benjamin Jesty (1736-1816) pioneered vaccination against smallpox after observing that if his milkmaids caught cowpox they were less likely to catch smallpox.

Robert Boyle's School of 1697 for 'twenty poor boys', Yetminster. The school owes its foundation to the the chemist's will, in which he left money for endowing three charities to be chosen by his executors, one of whom held land in Yetminster.

injecting cowpox germs into healthy people (starting with his wife and family).

Robert Boyle's school of 1697 is to be found at the west end of the village. In his will Boyle left provision for three charities which were chosen by his executors, and Boyles's school for twenty poor boys was built in Yetminster because one of his executors held land there. The school was absorbed into the County's School in 1947 but the endowment now provides books, equipment and sometimes clothing to secondary and further education students.

Yetminster on the little River Wriggle is an architectural delight. The local yellow limestone gives softness to the old, often date stoned buildings, while the neat rows of stone mullion windows look so timeless it is a shock to see that some of them have been blocked up against the window tax.

Church Farm and St Edwold's Church, Stockwood, lie at the foot of the chalk downs and mark the south-western edge of the Blackmore Vale. The lovely brick farmhouse is Georgian, but as well as being much more ancient the church is also the smallest in Dorset – 29ft 3in by 12ft 9in. The dedication is to the hermit brother of a Saxon king, who died in 971 and was buried at Cerne Abbas.

Well-kept cottages named to reveal the former trades carried on there, sympathetic modern infilling and early almond blossom against the old stones all make Yetminster a village not to be missed.

Leigh (pronounced Lie) has a pagan past connected with witchcraft. No doubt many other places in the Blackmore Vale have this also but Leigh's is well documented. In 1879 William Barnes gave the Dorset Field Club information gleaned many years before from a man who knew that a witches' sisterhood met on Leigh Common, and the last witch burned in England is said to have been arrested here.

There was once a Miz Maze at Leigh – low banks and trenches intricately arranged which local youths and girls would tread at holiday times. Hutchins said it was neglected by the 1770's. The enclosure is circular and small. Writing in 1906, Treves thought it unlikely to satisfy a generation that needed a barrel organ, a roundabout, swings, a row of coconuts and a fat woman in a tent to keep it amused. Many years ago every farm at Leigh had a cider orchard attached and knowledgeable cider drinkers considered Leigh's brew first class.

The road from Yeovil to Chetnole runs through marshy fields until they become flat and distinctly richer arable fields. If you go by train to Chetnole you have to ask the driver to stop at the tiny little Chetnole Halt right out in the fields. You will see signposts for Stockwood and the lyrically named Melbury Bubb with its 'tumbled hills' and Batcombe Ridge rising behind then. If you turn right, instead of left, when you come up from Chetnole railway halt you can walk to Stockwood (it can also be reached from here by footpaths). Here beside a farmhouse is a tiny church, the smallest in Dorset and one of the smallest in Britain, only 29 feet 3 inches long and 12 feet 9 inches wide. It is dedicated to Edwold, brother of King Edmund of East Anglia who was killed in battle. After his death Edwold came to Stockwood to become a hermit and died there.

However, you need to turn left and take a good walk along a quiet road to reach Chetnole village. My particular delight as I walked it last spring was the sight of a newly laid garden hedge laid by a consummate craftsman because, the owner told me, he was fed up with it being flailed and getting so thin.

Travellers in the past have noted the pretty well-kept gardens of the houses in the village and this enthusiasm for gardening is true of both old and new houses there today.

At the end of Mill Lane the little River Wriggle flows swiftly and clear. The Mill is now a well-preserved private house and across its gravelled front on the wall opposite there are some stone steps up the wall to facilitate a footpath.

There is considerable variety in the housebuilding styles of Chetnole – big Victorian bay windows, an iron porch, 1920's brick and timber houses and modern solar panels all make for an interesting exploration of the village. The mainly flagstoned Church of St. Peter is thought to have been a Christian church since Saxon times. Eventually following the success of the Crusades the Church became more militant and the building was enlarged. Much of it now is fifteenth century with a chancel and north aisle added in 1860.

THE SOUTH AND THE GREAT HILLS

Indomitable Holnest should not be missed, though it is so small now that it easily might be. The population of this undaunted little hamlet, thought to have been depopulated by the Black Death and never recovered, was 136 in 1901 and 87 in 1921.

The lovely little old church and graveyard are alone in the fields, though the scattered farming population works hard to keep the church open. It is in some ways a struggle for there have been several serious thefts from the fabric of the church. I never usually advocate the development of houses on green fields but wonder if here it might be useful, if only to protect the church?

The churchyard once had a huge and vulgar mausoleum (*see following page*) to a local squire John Drax (1800-1887), who after the death of his wife went to live at Holnest Lodge. Increasingly eccentric, he placed plaster statues of deities along the drive, then erected a sort of Nelson's column topped by a bronze statue of himself in a frock coat and holding a silk hat. That done, he built the mausoleum for himself in the 'supposedly Byzantine' style. It had marble pillars, bronze covered doors, stained glass windows and a Romanesque sarcophagus in the centre and it cost £10,000. It fell into decay and in 1935, a time of Art Deco design and economic depression, it was removed.

Culverhayes Manor House near the church, often called Dunn's Farm (now mostly seventeenth century), is said to have housed Benedictine monks from Sherborne Abbey who served the Church in the eleventh and twelfth centuries. They may have trained and influenced a young local boy named Stephen Harding, who was born at Sherborne in about the middle of the eleventh century and received his early education there before going on to study in Paris and Rome. He was later sent with a band of twenty monks to Citeaux to reform the new foundation there. His powers of organization were

The vast Byzantine Mausoleum in Holnest churchyard built for himself by the increasingly eccentric John Drax (1800-1887), which was demolished in 1935. Drax spent £10,000 on his mausoleum, which was completed long before his death. He even rehearsed his own funeral, shouting at his servants from inside his lead-lined coffin at every jolt and then sending it back to have it widened for his shoulders.

exceptional and the Cistercian order flourished. Stephen Harding became the third Abbot of Citeaux (1109-1133) but is regarded as the true founder of the order. Cistercian foundations expanded rapidly, especially fostering the wool and cloth trade in England, so that they are often regarded as the founders of her commercial prosperity.

A few years ago Holnest was much in the news when residents discovered that a field had been sold for a rubbish dump, not an ordinary rubbish dump but one to which French and German rubbish was to be imported by huge lorry load. Fortunately, protected great crested newts lived in a nearby pond and the newts, aided by the determined locals, saw off the scheme. They received support from all over the country and, when the scheme was rejected, Holnest and Glanville's Wootton bought the field from the Council. It is now a triple Area of Special Scientific Interest. The spot is still called Tip Field though.

Below Holnest Park sleepy little Hermitage at the foot of High Stoy gets its name from Augustinian monks who once lived there. It was thought that there was originally a hermit settlement in the heart of the Forest of Blackmore. This seems to have attracted so large a community that sometime in the reign of Henry III a rule similar to the friar hermits of St. Augustine was adopted, though not formally. The brethren placed themselves under the protection of the Earls of Cornwall, lords of the Forest, and their position was confirmed under Edward II in 1314. In 1325 the steward of the forest, Ingelram Berenger, made over to them 100 acres of land provided they should arrange to celebrate Mass daily in their church for the souls of Ingelram and the faithful departed, and to refresh ten mendicants once a day in the hermitage. Such records as there are give a fascinating glimpse of life in the deep forest of Blackmore at that time, and one cannot help feeling sorry that by 1349 all the inmates were dead. Eventually, the house became known as 'the free chapel of St. Mary', called the Hermitage, and passed into the custody of the master of the hospital of St. John at Dorchester, and later to the Abbot and convent of Cerne.

Glanville's Wootton (sometimes shown as Wootton Glanville) is a fine old mixture of a name from Old English 'Wudu-tu' (a homestead by a wood), and the Glanvilles from Glanville in Normandy who came there on the coat tails of the Conqueror. The fifteenth century church survived ferocious restoration in 1876.The west tower was fourteenth century and the chancel and nave fifteenth century, though the former was rebuilt in 1876 and the later extensively restored. Drawings are preserved in the faculty petition of 1875 in the Salisbury Diocesan archives, and there is still a lot to see that is old and beautiful. The oldest surviving part is the fourteenth century south chapel, thought to result from an endowment in 1344 by Sibyl de Glaunvyll who made provision for a chaplain to say mass daily at the altar. The south chapel is a notable example of fourteenth century architecture, with graceful pointed windows of three lights and an air of timeless serenity. There are some interesting floor slabs, monuments and tiles, the loveliest being to my mind the late

A drawing of the thirteenth century stone effigy in the
Church of St Mary, Glanville's Wootton.

thirteenth century recumbent stone effigy of a man, a slight figure
wearing a long, military-like surcoat with short sleeves, tippet and
hood. A dagger and sword are slung from a belt buckled over the
hips, but his face expresses calm of mind and his hair lies in a
surprisingly modern off-the-face pageboy style.

The late Elizabethan Round Chimneys Farmhouse, once called
Newlands, lies well north of the parish church. Hutchins shows the
main block with a gabled and dormer windowed third storey, but it
has only two storeys now. It was originally a manor house and was
the home of John Churchill (died 1652) and his son Winston (died
1688), the grandfather and father respectively of John Churchill the
first Duke of Marlborough, to whom the grateful nation presented
Blenheim Palace.

On Dungeon Hill, part of the scattered village of Buckland
Newton, a Roman encampment once extended over eleven acres and
Roman military relics are sometimes ploughed up there. Buckland
Newton with its outlying hamlets and farms has no less than five
different foundations – chalk, greensand, limestone, Kimmeridge
Clay and Oxford Clay. It lies on the edge of the Blackmore Vale,
disposed among hillocks and hollows. Buckland comes from the
Saxon 'Bocland' – land granted under charter by the king – and
traditional goose fairs and sales of small animals take place there
regularly.

Throughout the Middle Ages Glastonbury Abbey, which held
estates there, concentrated on raising sheep and sheep farming

continued in the area with, as an early twentieth traveller put it, 'pasture all the way, scarcely relieved by the sight of a single piece of arable'.

The Church of the Holy Rood at Buckland Newton is rendered, which sits oddly in the landscape, and Ralph Wightman said it reminded him of a French Foreign Legion fort. However, it has some interesting stone fragments, notably a seventh or eighth century warrior and a twelfth century sculpture representing Christ in Majesty. There is also a remarkable sixteenth century carved poor box three feet high. The chancel of the church is largely thirteenth century and its windows are considered unusually fine for a country church of that date. There is a tablet to Thomas Barnes describing him as 'a man of sound understanding, a prudent mind. a lover of the holy faith' – as was his descendant the poet William.

The spelling of the village of Kings Stag seems to vary. On signposts it is spelt King Stag, whilst some guide books give it as Kingstag. Despite the variations in spelling, it is quite probable that the little place owes its name to King's 'Stake', a boundary stake marking the place where the parishes of Lydlinch, Pulham and Hazelbury Bryan meet. Less prosaically, legend has it that Henry III, out hunting in the Vale, came upon a beautiful white hart and was so impressed with its beauty that he spared its life. Some time later, however, his bailiff Sir Thomas de la Lynde found the same white hart in the woods, hunted it to a spot beside a bridge over the River

The drawing from Hutchins *History of Dorset* of Round Chimneys Farmhouse, Glanville's Wootton. The Elizabethan manor house was the birthplace of John Churchill, 1st Duke of Marlborough.

King's Stag Bridge over the River Lydden near Pulham. According to legend, the bridge is where Henry III's bailiff of the Royal Forest of Blackmore killed a white hart already spared by the king, with the result that a tax called White Hart Silver was levied on the area.

Lydden and killed it there. When the king learned of this, he was so furious that he threw the unfortunate Sir Thomas into prison, and levied a tax on the land around, known as White Hart Silver. Thereafter the Vale became known as the Vale of the White Hart and the descendants of Sir Thomas de la Lynde bore as their arms 'three harts' heads in a field gules'. Whatever the truth, there is evidence that a tax called White Hart Silver was levied, and surly squires and yeomen had to pay it. Moreover, the bridge in the parish of Pulham where the hart was said to have been killed is known as King's Stag Bridge.

Pulham's Grange Farm is recorded by 1327 as the Grange of the Abbot of Bindon. There is a sturdy eighteenth century rectory and the church is dedicated, like nearby Lydlinch, to St. Thomas à Becket. It was where in the evening of Victory in Europe Day (8th May 1945) everyone in the village from young mums pushing prams to a pigman in his 'piggy' boots left what they were doing and to the sound at last of church bells, flocked to church, to give thanks to God.

The White Hart has given its name to the pub at Bishop's Caundle, but not at Pulham where the pub is called The Green Man. The Green Man may be a symbol of a forester or of a forest spirit placed within churches to remind Christians of both the ancient woodlands felled to establish monastic settlements and the earthy pagan religion

The 'green man' in the Church of St Peter and St Paul, Mappowder.
The stone cottage by the church gate was the home of the novelist Theodore
Powys (1875-1953), author of *Mr Weston's Good Wine*.

banished along with the trees. In the parish church at Mappowder
there is an arcade of three uniform two-centred arches. On one of
these, just below the springing, there is a carved bracket representing
a human mask. He has a slack, ugly mouth and narrowed eyes, while
from his nostrils sprout wide carved leaves. He too is a Green Man.
Whatever the explanation for this symbol, the land around Pulham is
mostly good dairying country.

A few miles from Pulham there are two more Fifeheads – Fifehead
Neville and Fifehead St. Quintin. 'Neville' comes from William de
Nevil from Neuville in Normandy. Fifehead St. Quintin is small now,
the principal building being Lower Fifehead Farm with beautiful
stone-mullioned windows in a basically sixteenth century building.
Hutchins describes this as 'anciently a manor, now a farm and the St.
Quintins as 'an ancient and noble family'.

At Fifehead Neville a Roman mosaic pavement was excavated in
1881 and again in 1902–1905. In the course of these, some rather
fine mosaic tiles were discovered and a horde of rings, bracelets and
brooches unearthed. The rings were marked with the chi-rho
Christian symbol and one is patterned with a dove and olive
branches. Some of the find is in the Dorset County Museum and the
rest in the British Museum.

The medieval packhorse bridge over the River Divelish at Fifehead Neville.

There is a bridge over the little River Divelish. William Barnes relates how when he was a small boy his mother, who came from Fifehead Neville, took him to see the 'Roman figures' on the bridge. They are gone now and the bridge, which was probably medieval, may have been much restored. It is a packhorse bridge with two pointed arches (which is unusual). The steep, well-trodden path over the bridge must have carried laden packhorses for centuries. The bridge has a fairly modern looking rail now (thank goodness) for below it is a fast-flowing water splash into a deep pool of the river: a highways notice says 'Ford' but such places are called 'Water Splashes' in the Blackmore Vale.

At the mill house there is a red roofed stone building which must have housed the working mill, with the white miller's house by the road. Monica Hutchings relates how, the day after a very bad cloudburst in 1955 caused violent flooding, she called at the mill and learned that all the livestock and poultry had been swept away.

Fifehead Neville church is not to be missed. It is small, tucked in among old swaying yew trees and obviously greatly loved. It was altered and made classical in 1736 and more work was done to it in the nineteenth century, but the floor is entirely of creamy slabs and parquet – no garish tiles.

Here Roger Goodfellow left the rent of a meadow for the relief of 'the second poor' (people who were necessitous but not in receipt of parish relief). Here too the little church was once lighted by oil lamps which were turfed out, rediscovered in the Church Hall and restored in 1976 with electricity so that they are perfectly in keeping with the church.

I love the name Hazelbury Bryan. It makes one want to sing it but the church and school are in an area called Droop, which makes one want to catch one's breath or sing flat. The church is mainly fifteen century with some lovely tracery lights of that period. It is obviously loved and the lectern has black oak in its design. The oak comes from a Roman bridge at Newcastle and the oak tree would have been living when Jesus was on earth.

The lych-gate provided by Miss Violet Cross won a Civic Trust award. Miss Cross, who died in 1989 aged 98, magistrate, County Councillor, patron of charities and conserver of old buildings, lived in Hazelbury Bryan at the manor house for many years. She had been matron of a field hospital in France in the First World War and returned there in 1940. Caught and interrogated by the advancing German army, she managed, by lucky chance, to convince her captors that she was a Portuguese peasant, reached Lisbon, got a lift on a

Violet Cross was one of the great figures of Hazelbury Bryan until her death in 1989 aged 98. She was awarded the Croix de Guerre for her ambulance work during the First World War, only to be captured by the Germans in France in 1940. Freed after convincing her interrogators that she was Portugese, she hitched a lift on a flying boat from Lisbon to Poole, finally walking the 25 miles home to Hazelbury Bryan.

flying boat as far as Poole Harbour, then walked the twenty five miles home to Hazelbury Bryan. I was lucky enough to hear her speak about her experiences and remember shaking with fear and excitement as she did so.

Hazelbury Bryan is a delight to the eye with old granaries, barns and staddle stones and on one house an iron porch with glass door and crimson borders to the panes. The fields are much more open here and less like Hardy's 'mere paddocks' as they roll towards the great hills, notably Bulbarrow.

Mappowder takes its name from the old English 'mapulder' or'mapuldor' – a maple tree. The village was named by John Claridge in 1730 as the southernmost limit of the Blackmore Vale and others have thought it a Dorset village that has changed little over the centuries. In a recess in the much restored church there is a little mid thirteenth century stone effigy (eighteen inches long) of a knight in mail with shield and sword and his feet resting on a couched lion to signify death in the Holy Land.

The lion has a forthcoming, enquiring look about it and to my mind it bears a distinct resemblance to the lion under the crusader's feet in the little church at Stock Gaylard. One cannot help wondering why men left the (relative) comfort and safety of the Blackmore Vale some seven hundred and fifty years ago to join Crusades? It was surely more than a wish to preserve the holy places of Christianity from the infidel? Whatever their motives, some think they started the unrest in the Middle East that is still with us today.

Stoke Wake lies just below the great Bulbarrow Hill and the Celtic camp of Rawlesbury which juts out above the village. The view from these parts to the north and north east says Hutchins 'surpasses all imagination'. He is right. It does. Because of its position, the tiny village is difficult to find. There was an old church there which was replaced in 1872 by a new one and which, in turn, is now a farm building.

Woolland, a spring-line settlement in a green bowl just below Woolland Hill lies on a steep escarpment. It is said to be 900 feet above sea level at the summit. Traces remain of Celtic fields both here and at nearby Ibberton, but they have been greatly damaged by ploughing. In the churchyard there is a huge old yew tree which has

The brass of 1616 to Mary Argenton in the north chapel of
Woolland church – 'here lyeth our Landladie, loved of all.'

been proven to be 2000 years old. The church was completely rebuilt
in Victorian times but still retains a lovely brass of Mary Argenton in
ruff and farthingale who died in 1616. She was the mistress of the
manor:

> 'The revenew whereof, she freelye did spend
> In good hospitalitie until her lives end'.

You need to be fit to make the steep climb to Ibberton Church
which is, unusually, dedicated to St. Eustacius or Eustace. At the
bottom of the hill a notice on a gate threatens you with a fine if you
leave it unlocked, but as the fine is for forty shillings the notice
probably began life on a railway crossing. The last time I made the
climb I found white violets with their heavenly scent on a bank at the
bottom.

You climb up by either a steep, sandy, rutted lane or a flight of old
mossy stone steps. The lane is wide enough for a hand or horse-
drawn bier, but can a modern motor hearse get up there? The old
door is fastened with a long wooden latch and there is no stained

glass, except for the Arms of Elizabeth I in slightly battered glass, giving the church a feeling of great age and peace.

The view of the Vale from the church is superb and the lane is said to go on to connect at the top of the deeply wooded hill with Iron Age trackways. The wonderful situation of this church inspires lyricism, notably in Treves who, recording that someone long ago gave an acre of land here for the ringing of the morning bell, exhorts the reader to, imagine the hamlet on a May morning 'when cottage windows are being thrown open to the sun and at such hour hear floating down from the silent hill the greeting of the morning bell'.

The little hamlet of Belchalwell gets its name from several old English words – 'belle' meaning a hill and 'ceald-well', a cold stream. There are more lovely views here, especially from the hill that the church sits on. The Blackmore Vale is spread out below to the west and on fine warm days one gets a good view of hang gliders coming off Bulbarrow. The church is a plain stone building with a square embattled tower, but some of the gargoyles are a delight. One looks like a sheep with a man's face. The church has a fine Norman porch, a chancel, nave and north aisle.

The church was badly treated, the interior virtually destroyed by the Puritans who found this remote place and wreaked such havoc on the defenceless little church that only a patch of former wall painting remains to show the vibrant colour there must once have been.

Misfortune befell it again when all its records were burnt in a fire in Blandford. This meant that the dedication was lost along with the records, so in 1959 it was decided to dedicate the church to St. Aldhelm. This is a happy choice. Aldhelm, a deeply learned man, became the first Bishop of the newly created West Saxon diocese, with Sherborne as its seat. Bishop Aldhelm was by all accounts a lovely man, tall and sturdy with an ash staff in his hand and a harp slung over his shoulder. He walked tirelessly about his diocese and when he and his monks stopped for a rest, Aldhelm would play and sing popular songs to them, or songs of his own composition, charming all who heard him. Did the learned, gentle Saint Aldhelm ever come to lovely Belchalwell I wonder? I hope he did for he would have appreciated its beauty.

PRESERVING THE VALE

Let other vo'k meäke money väster
In the air o' dark-room'd towns,
I don't dread a peevish meäster;
Though noo man do heed my frowns,
I be free to go abrode,
Or teäke ageän my hwomeward road
To where, vor me, the apple tree
Do leän do low in Linden Lea

'My Orchard in Linden Lea', WILLIAM BARNES

Those who are born and bred in the Blackmore Vale often develop the deepest love for it and are assailed by gnawing homesickness like a undrawn tooth until they can return.

Newcomers to the Vale are taken with its beauty and with its slowness – the sense of an older England that did not quite get lost because the Industrial Revolution passed it by.

The Blackmore Vale attracts tourists from all over the world, but this is an age of ruthless conformity when historic market towns are being stuffed with supermarkets, multiples and chain stores so that every town, and its merchandise, look exactly the same. So can we protect the unique qualities of this lovely Vale?

Change there must inevitably be. We cannot freeze the landscape and way of life in a time warp. This is just not possible or desirable. Farming methods have changed so much from their mid-Victorian heyday when rows of milkmaids sat on three legged stools and milked cows with names like Happy and Daisy.

Small farms have been relentlessly amalgamated into larger units and, in 2003, sixty per cent of farm sales were to new non-farming owners, people who did not intend to farm their land. At the same time, the organic farming movement is gaining in strength. Increased leisure adds to the attendance at agricultural shows, point-to-point and race meetings and the demand for stabling and training for horses. Increased tourism demands additional holiday accommodation.

Fortunately, the tremendous growth of the heritage and conservation movements in recent years, a reaction to the 'bash it all down and build something new' mentality of the 1960's, has created a climate that will help the Blackmore Vale. The Local Authority recognizes a clear need for restraint policies to protect important landscapes, the local ecology and the best quality agricultural land.

Unfortunately, the local authority may not get support from Central Government. This is so with wind farms, a problem in the Blackmore Vale as I write. Central Government is committed to increasing energy from renewable sources, so there is pressure on local authorities to allow them on the fringes of Areas of Outstanding Natural Beauty while residents, of course, resent both the spoliation of the landscape and the loss of value of their properties. In any case, wind turbines emit considerable noise and are often not considered an efficient way of providing energy.

In the same way, Local Authorities may wish to preserve the landscape and prevent building on green field sites, but they are directed by Central Government to provide many thousands of 'new homes'. The Blackmore Vale, because it has never been industrialized, cannot provide many brownfield sites, only priceless and richly beautiful green fields.

It may be in the end that the only way to protect the Vale will be to organize protests and marches and lodge ourselves in the trees. If you have enjoyed discovering this beautiful Blackmore Vale, I hope you will come with us!

FURTHER READING

Barnes, William, *William Barnes, The Dorset Poet, A Comprehensive Selection of Poetry & Prose* (ed. Chris Wrigley (1984)
Bettey, J.H., *Dorset* (1972)
Chedzoy, Alan, *William Barnes, A Life of the Dorset Poet* (1985)
Draper, Jo, *Dorset, The Complete Guide* (1986)
Gant, R, *Dorset Villages* (1980)
Gardiner, Dorothy, *Companion into Dorset* (1937)
Hutchins, John, *The History and Antiquities of the County of Dorset* (3rd edition, 4 vols 1861-1870)
Hutchins, Monica, *Dorset River* (1956)
  Inside Dorset (1965)
HMSO, *Historical Monuments in the County of Dorset,* vol III 'Central' (1970), vol IV 'North' (1972)
Silton WI, *Silton, Records of a Dorset Village* (1999)
The Marnhull Festival of Britain Committee, *The Marn'll Book* (1952)
Powys, Llewellyn, *Dorset Essays* (1935)
Treves, Frederick, *Highways and Byways in Dorset* (1906)
Wightman, Ralph, *Portrait of Dorset* (1965)

ACKNOWLEDGEMENTS

Most of the photographs and other illustrations are taken from the collections of the author and the Dovecote Press, but Hilary Townsend would like to thank the following for allowing the inclusion of illustrations in their possession or for which they hold the copyright: Dorset County Museum; pages 16 (bottom), 18, 24, 72, 79: Dorset Life/Peter Booton; page 55: Philip Knott; page 61: Royal Commission Historical Monuments (England) © Crown Copyright; pages 11 (bottom), 13 (right), 28, 29, 48, 63: Tate Gallery, London; page 41: W.J. White; page 13 (left). The brass of Mary Argenton in Woolland Church is taken from *Dorset Brasses* by Doris Sibun, published in 1974.

INDEX

The

DISCOVER DORSET

Series of Books

A series of paperback books providing informative illustrated
introductions to Dorset's history, culture and way of life.
The following titles have so far been published.

All the books about Dorset published by The Dovecote Press
are available in bookshops throughout the county,
or in case of difficulty direct from the publishers.
The Dovecote Press Ltd, Stanbridge,
Wimborne, Dorset BH21 4JD
Tel: 01258 840549 www.dovecotepress.com